The Road to the Kingdom.

How to awaken the King and Queen within.

By Joseph Anthony Campbell

Road to the Kingdom Copyright © 2019 by Joseph Anthony Campbell. All Rights Reserved.

All rights reserved. No part of this book may be reproduced in any form or by any electronic or mechanical means including information storage and retrieval systems, without permission in writing from the author. The only exception is by a reviewer, who may quote short excerpts in a review.

Names, characters, places, and incidents either are products of the author's imagination or are used fictitiously. Any resemblance to actual persons, living or dead, events, or locales is entirely coincidental.

Joseph Anthony Campbell.
Contact me at josephrtk@gmail.com

First Printing: Jan 2019.

Dedicated with love to my Mother Marian Campbell and my late 'Nana' Frances Parrett, without whom this book would certainly not be possible.

"The ability to love and nurture began with the mother's warmth, the mother's love."

A new commandment I give to you, that you love one another: just as I have loved you, you also are to love one another.

JOHN 13:34 (NEW REVISED STANDARD VERSION)

The Road to the Kingdom.

About the Author.

Thank you for beginning to read this book. In terms of myself, I am forty years of age and I have travelled extensively and journalled prolifically on my own "Road to the Kingdom". I have overcome personal issues as per the subject of this book and experienced a transformation through applying its principles; which I do daily. I am from Liverpool, England and I have lived and worked in London for the last eleven years (although I do love visiting California when I can.)

In terms of my past, twenty years ago I won my private college's creative writing award 'The G.E. Alston award' presented in Liverpool Cathedral. I also graduated with honours from the Universities of Liverpool and Leeds in English Literature and Philosophy. I also graduated from my teacher training at the University of Liverpool to teach English Literature and Drama with first class honours. I have been a holiday representative in Ibiza, a singer in England, Spain and Australia and I have taught Musical theatre in the United States. I have also written songs and poetry and I also became a member of Spotlight and Equity and I am a member of the Actor's Centre in London.

Currently, I have taught and I have provided private tuition for over 15 years up to and including University level English Literature, English Language, Religious Studies, Drama, Creative Writing, Sociology, Philosophy and Psychology. I am a practicing life coach and I am currently training to be a psychotherapist and therapeutic counsellor.

By Joseph Anthony Campbell

As a writer I have written academic resources for the Times Educational supplement and I now concentrate my full energies on my writing/teaching/Life coaching and counselling. I am constantly learning, partaking in courses all over the world and this book is the distillation of the best knowledge I can pass on from all the time I have been alive and particularly from the last twenty-five years of my life.

Excitingly, in Summer 2019 from the 19th of July to the 8th of September I will be running both weekend and three-day "Road to the Kingdom" courses in central London. Contact me at josephrtk@gmail.com to register your interest in taking part and to get great early bird offers on the courses taking place in central London.

I look forward to traveling the Road to the Kingdom together with you.

Author's note.

The Road to the Kingdom is a self-help book that describes a number of stages or steps that take place on the journey to the 'Kingdom'.

We start in the 'Wilderness', and receive an inner call to leave (for our death on some level is close at hand, perhaps even literal, physical death) and events occur which could be ascribed as a call to adventure, a call to begin our journey; our 'Road to the Kingdom'.

Do you dare to follow your calling?

If you accept the call to journey upon the 'Road to the Kingdom' you must face tasks and trials. We ultimately have to face our fears before our severest challenge, an ultimate 'Final Battle'. First, we develop the skills needed in stages, training in developing the archetypal skills and ideal traits of the archetypal images of the 'Magician', 'Warrior' and 'Lover' before ultimately embodying the 'King' or 'Queen' within.

This book is for those who strive to meet their destiny and who want to ascend to their highest level of being.

By Joseph Anthony Campbell

A note on the spiritual aspects of this book and how it is structured.

The Road to the Kingdom is presented in the style of an actual handbook for a Templar or Paladin but it is addressed to all readers. It is presented as a guide to experiencing a form of spiritual enlightenment also and stresses the importance of living in the present moment; in the 'NOW'.

It is a collection of teachings and the enclosing narrative is presented whereby on every page there is an inspirational thought, which can be read as a part of the whole book's philosophy or it can be used to form the basis of a meditation.

The book draws from a variety of spiritual traditions. The Road to the Kingdom contains aphorisms that have a specific spiritual source also such as Lao Tzu and Jesus in order to provide spiritual inspiration. The book also further describes methods of meditation to aid readers in anchoring themselves spiritually. These methods include focusing on your goal, (The Kingdom) and spending time in nature. After each passage the reader may then reflect and become still.

The Road to the Kingdom.

Contents

About the Author. 5
Author's note. 7
A note on the spiritual aspects of this book and how it is structured. 8
Contents 9
Chapter 1: Wilderness. 13
The Journey begins in the Wilderness. 14
The Days of Dust. 15
We often fight demons from our childhood..16
We begin to eliminate the juvenile or even childish features we have. 17
Wounds are important! 18
Fighting upstream against life's current. 19
Appreciation of our weaknesses. 20
I cannot change what I have done, said or felt...21
  We had always been, were now and forever would be, powerless over the deeds and motives of others. 22
  If we fully accept that we cannot control others, then and only then can we look at what controls us. 23
    Hidden treasures. 24
    The power of your name...25
    We now experience the magnificence of our own solitude. 26
    Training is important..27
    Carl Jung created archetypes for the male and female personality. 28
    The Samurai culture were well versed in Poetry, Literature, Philosophy and even flower arranging..29
    Emerging from the Wilderness. Our training begins. 30
    Chapter 2: We develop the Magician within us...31
Accept what you cannot change; change the things you can. 32
Acceptance of our past decisions. 33
Accept indifference or even contempt from others along the Road. 34
When others doubt us! 35
At times we act despite a lack of faith. 36
Denying temptation. 37

Accepting responsibility for yourself and for others. 38
We tell the truth despite the consequences we may incur. 39
Help from others may come from those you have helped previously. 40
We learn from and honour those who have attained the Kingdom. 41
Letting people go. 42
There is always hope! 43
Trust, Hope and Persevere. 44
We concentrate on our efforts rather than the outcome. 45
The average person lives for approximately 28000 days. 46
Those who say the Kingdom cannot be achieved are interrupting those who are achieving it. 47
  Chapter 3: We develop the Lover within us. 48
  Trust in Love. 49
  Although love is undeniably a feeling it is ultimately a choice. 50
  We are to love one another. 51
  Love is inexhaustible. 52
  Saying goodbye to those we love. 53
  Concern for those we love above ourselves. 54
  We have an appreciation of the feminine and masculine in our lives. 55
  Provide children with love and safety. 56
  Be the light that renews. 57
There is nothing on Earth that we can relate to more fundamentally than another human being. 58
  Be quick to forgive. 59
  We have an affinity with animals and nature. 60
  We are grateful. 61
  We are kind to others. 62
  Wishing joy for others. 63
  We aim to help those who have been damaged by the past. 64
People are not to be used for the love of money; money is to be used to love people. 65
The ability to love and nurture began with the mother's warmth, the mother's love. 66
  We minister to the sick. 67
  We help others even when we are in need. 68
  We acknowledge and honour those who are often overlooked. 69
  We have a gentle and firm way. 70
  We are becoming humble. 71
  We have an appreciation for the beauty of our existence. 72
  We have an appreciation of History and our ancestors. 73

The Road to the Kingdom.

We honour other cultures. 74
We speak well of others. 75
Love and tolerance. 76
Chapter 4: We develop the Warrior within us. 77
Do not stand down. Do not stand aside. Do not stand against. Stand up! 78
We now reflect and respond rather than react. 79
Life is 10% what happens to you and 90% how you respond to it. 80
Offering our hand even if it may be refused. 81
The Road to the Kingdom involves courage, benevolence and decisiveness. 82
Patience and discipline. 83
Courage determines the quality of your life. 84
The Hunt. 85
We keep our sword sharp. 86
We endure when we must in order to survive. 87
Defeats along the Road. 88
Do not doubt your faith; doubt your doubt. 89
Protecting with our very lives. 90
Knowing *when* to take action. 91
Embracing the moment for leadership. 92
Protecting the vulnerable. 93
Maintaining hope, no matter what we are facing. 94
Face your fears and difficulties. 95
Ride out and meet the enemy. 96
Chapter 5: We journey upon The Road to the Kingdom. 97
We now have the necessary understanding. 98
After training, we act. 99
We take the Road and follow it until its final destination; the Kingdom. 100
We are restoring a broken lineage. 101
Our past does not equal our future. 102
We acknowledge our qualities. 103
We accept the praise of mentors. 104
Our weakness is becoming our strength. 105
A personal destiny has emerged. 106
We made a concrete decision to follow The Road to the Kingdom. 107
At times we experienced supernatural help. 108
Chapter 6: We reflect upon Spiritual truths before our Final Battle. 109
We must seek out the Power that is greater than all things. 110
All words are mere pointers to a transcendent reality. 111
Life is always now. 112
Accept everything as it is. 113

Non-resistance, non-judgment and non-attachment...114
The Road to the Kingdom is a Spiritual journey. 115
The Road to faith is a deeply personal journey. 116
We accept that God made this Road. 117
We are always loved and protected. 118
Be prepared to let go of all that you fear to lose...119
Chapter 7: We embark upon our Final Battle..120
Become who you were born to be. 121
Our time has come; this is our destiny!...122
We charge into the mouth of the darkness. 123
Death is an illusion..124
Chapter 8: Realising the Kingdom. 125
We had met ourselves and found ourselves worthy..126
When the crownless become Kings and Queens. 127
We will rejoin those we have lost..128
We are all one..129
We kneel to the Source. 130
Epilogue. 131
Summer courses 2019!..132
A final message to you; dearest reader..134

The Road to the Kingdom.

Chapter 1: Wilderness.

By Joseph Anthony Campbell

The Journey begins in the Wilderness.

What sent you into the Wilderness
    What event or events in your past?
    For there can be no mistake. The Wilderness is where you are. But it is not who you are.
    You may experience it as mild discomfort or a place full of the bones of the dead. The detritus all around you.
    Here, there is no light. We will all experience this place, this darkness.
    We cannot stay. We must climb back into the light.
    However, this time and place must be experienced.
    It provides us with a memory that we must preserve.
    The memory serves us.
    It serves as a reminder if we find ourselves gradually returning to the Wilderness once we have been freed.
    However, make no mistake, the journey begins here.
    At the precipice.
    At the very jaws of death.
    The light but a dim spark in the distance.

The Days of Dust.

The days of dust are a time of ashes.

In tribal times, young men would sometimes roll around the ashes in their tribal hut. They would even eat the ashes.

All young people experience this in varying forms.

In Biblical times they would repent with "sackcloth and ashes". [1]

To mourn the dead, to repent, to be delivered.

Here in the days of dust.

Here at this time of ashes.

Our "Katabasis" begins. (This is the Greek word for a descent.)

For us to return as a living revenant, we must experience our death in some form.

At the apex of our descent, we begin our return.

We make the first steps of our ascent.

---

[1] Esther 4:1 (New Revised Standard Version)

By Joseph Anthony Campbell

We often fight demons from our childhood.

We often fight demons from our childhood and our juvenile years.
We may be struggling from wounds placed by our Mother our substitute Mother's (real and imaginary).

    Often, we are struggling from wounds placed by our actual Father or substitute Fathers (real and imaginary).

    The wounds placed by our Fathers are often profound.
    For our Fathers may have been our substitutes for God.
    Fathers cannot live up to this unrealistic expectation.
    Mothers cannot either.
    The problem with your childhood may be that it has lasted too long.
    We must forgive. We must take responsibility for our own lives.
    We may, at this time, be juvenile.
    We may, at this time, even be childish.

We begin to eliminate the juvenile or even childish features we have.

We begin to eliminate the juvenile or even childish features we have carried into our adulthood.

To retain juvenile features into adulthood is called neoteny. It is not a natural process.

It is or was an unnatural occurrence.
This means that we have not developed into a complete person.
This means that we have not developed into the King or Queen that we are.
Instead, many of us feel an invisible barrier to becoming whole.
Many of us are locked out of the Kingdom.
You can obtain the keys to this Kingdom.
It is the right manifestation of ourselves that will enter the Kingdom.
Within you are the seeds of wholeness!

By Joseph Anthony Campbell

Wounds are important!

The scar tissue of our past is a strong symbol.
Pain is a part of our lives; it becomes a marker for our progress.
Make a decision; I am going to grow through it, rather than go through it.
Your past shaped your attitudes.
Your suffering shaped your character.
Your past has led you to this exact moment.
This quintessential, constantly fleeting, momentary reality.
The pain of the Wilderness is leading to the dawn of understanding.
You are becoming free of your pain.
Without pain we can experience no lasting change.
Our wounds heal.
Our scar tissue serves as a reminder of the Wilderness.
It is a symbol of the pain inflicted by the Wilderness.

Fighting upstream against life's current.

Fighting upstream against life's current, we learned that when we resist life, life resists us.

What we resist; persists.

As we shatter ourselves against the rocks of our reality, we begin to learn to be in alignment with life itself.

We learn where the rocks are.

We accept our inevitable shattering; we avoid it when we can.

Accept this moment.

Accept the current and flow in its direction.

Allow life to be and live according to the flow of its current.

Life mirrors our actions.

The world cannot make you complete; only you can.

Accept the current, accept life and see what happens.

A paradigm shift in your reality awaits.

By Joseph Anthony Campbell

Appreciation of our weaknesses.

Appreciation of our weaknesses is fundamental.
    Our overlooking them or denial of them may have led us to the Wilderness.
    They may have brought us close to death.
    We may have generational illnesses in the form of addictions.
    We therefore begin the process of freeing ourselves from our addictions.
    Hurt people, hurt people. Thus, we begin reversing this vicious cycle.
    We do not partake in our chosen addiction.
    We follow this path to its conclusion.
    We get the help we need.
    You may find you are enchained.
    Therefore, we also focus on that which is free within us. We know that when we do this, we will affect what is entrapped to eventually be liberated.

I cannot change what I have done, said or felt.

I cannot change what I have done, said or felt. I can only move forward with my life.
    Here, in the Wilderness, we realise this salient truth.
    The past is finished. It is always finished.
    It is an illusion.
    A thought only.
    A thought I only ever have in the present.
    We assess our current situation. What we have done, we have done.
    Our past feelings and words too have no bearing on the present.
    The pristine present.
    We assess our current situation. We cannot go back; we cannot project towards the phantasm that is the future.
    We move forward with our lives.
    We move forward and we do it now!

By Joseph Anthony Campbell

We had always been, were now and forever would be, powerless over the deeds and motives of others.

We had always been, were now and forever would be, powerless over the deeds and motives of others.

We have sought others approval. We have attempted, some of us vigorously, to control others.

To control their deeds, to seek out their motives.

This had failed us in the past, it fails us now and it will forever fail.

We are powerless over others.

We need to fully understand this.

This truth will enable us to begin to emerge from the Wilderness.

Control of ourselves is possible to some extent but we do not control others.

Once we accept our powerlessness over others, we can work on that which we can control in ourselves.

> *If we fully accept that we cannot control others, then and only then can we look at what controls us.*

If we fully accept that we cannot control others, then and only then can we look at what controls us.

Our thoughts and our feelings make up our existence.

Thoughts appear, in the meaning making machine that is our brain, which we experience as a mind. Or, even worse, we experience it as who we believe we are.

Establishing a concept of self, of ourselves from our thoughts, can be entirely destructive.

Our thoughts are conditioned by the past.

Our thoughts are often useless.

We need to guide and direct our thoughts, when needed.

Most of all, we need to be able to switch them off when necessary.

Where our thoughts go, our emotions follow.

If we learn to both direct and diminish our thoughts and emotions, we will change our reality.

We will change what we are able to control.

By Joseph Anthony Campbell

Hidden treasures.

Hidden treasures can be found in the positive things that others have said, done and given to us.

These treasures can sustain us whilst we are in the Wilderness.

These words, actions and memories of encouragement can counteract the pain we feel.

We are beginning the process of emerging from the Wilderness.

We are taking the steps necessary to rebuild ourselves.

We have noted our weaknesses, now we must also analyse our strengths.

Analyse them accurately.

The darker the cave, the more important the treasure within.

We are emerging from a cave that had no light.

No light but a dim spark in the distance.

The dim spark of light grows brighter.

The power of your name.

The power of your name.

There is power within your name.

You will only ever have one name and it is yours. Yours to own.

There are hidden treasures contained within our names.

For example, the apparently common name of Paul which originally meant 'servant' has gold within the middle of the name, as the chemical symbol for Gold is 'Au'.

We can walk around unaware of the Gold within our names and the Kingdom that is within our very blood. Within our very self.

The Wilderness has made us nameless. It has made our lives meaningless.

My name is Joseph. Joseph means "God will increase".

I reclaim my name. I reclaim its meaning.

It is time to reclaim our names.

It is time to reclaim their meaning.

By Joseph Anthony Campbell

We now experience the magnificence of our own solitude.

We now experience the magnificence of our own solitude and begin to develop a well-spring of inner dignity and wholeness.

We are making the beginnings of a recovery.

We are developing some internal strength.

As within, so without.

Our brokenness is diminishing. We are beginning our journey towards completion.

In the magnificence of our own company we have made an honest assessment of our strengths and our weaknesses.

There are many more lessons to learn.

We must leave this Wilderness. This torrid place.

There is a strange reticence to emerge from the familiarity of the Wilderness.

One glance at our scars however reminds us of our pressing need to leave this place.

We know that we have much training to do before we can emerge upon the Road to the Kingdom.

The Road to the Kingdom.

Training is important.

Training is important.
    The Wilderness can be a place to hide.
    The Wilderness can be a place to die.
    We have used the Wilderness as a place to lay a foundation.
    A foundation to learn the skills required for the Road ahead.
    The Road that will lead us to the Kingdom.
    Our training will be physical, mental and emotional.
    We have quietly read and learnt whilst in the Wilderness.
    We are beginning to learn the meaning of humility.
    We now emerge from the Wilderness.
    We are ready to begin the next stage of our journey.
    Our training is about to begin.

By Joseph Anthony Campbell

Carl Jung created archetypes for the male and female personality.

Carl Jung created archetypes for the male and female personality.

This was developed by Robert L. Moore into the King (Queen), Warrior, Lover and Magician model.

This model is demonstrated throughout history.

In the 15th century the Renaissance man (perhaps most brilliantly exemplified by Leonardo Da Vinci) was to develop all his skills, particularly as a soldier (Warrior), scholar (Magician) and courtier (Lover).

This model is entirely adaptable to women, as we have discerned throughout the ages.

Notable examples are also found in Medieval Japan through both the Samurai and Ninja cultures that practiced Bushido and Ninjutsu.

The 12th Century Knights Templar also provides us with an excellent example of this model.

> *The Samurai culture were well versed in Poetry, Literature, Philosophy and even flower arranging.*

The Samurai culture were well versed in Poetry, Literature, Philosophy and even flower arranging.

They were also noted for their excellent swordsmanship as elite warriors, as noted in Bushido 'Way of the Warrior'[2].

Ninjutsu was practiced by Ninjas who were also noted warriors and elite magicians through their training in disguise, escape, concealment, geography, meteorology, medicine, and explosives.

Ninjas and Samurai were Warriors, Lovers and Magicians.

The 12th century Knights Templar bravely fought for a noble purpose; to protect religious pilgrims to Jerusalem from murderous attacks.

Their fight for 'good' in its purest form was not to garner accolades but because it was an integral part of their nature to do 'good'.

They were both Warrior and Lover.

Warrior poets are found throughout Literature and History.

---

[2]Tsunetomo, Yamamoto, *Bushido: The Way of the Samurai* (Square One Classics) (1 Oct. 2001)

By Joseph Anthony Campbell

Emerging from the Wilderness.
Our training begins.

Emerging from the Wilderness. Our training begins.

We now journey into deepening our skills as Magicians, Lovers and Warriors.

This is vital in preparation for our journey. Vital in order to discover what is deep within us; the Kingdom.

We need to deepen our understanding of these archetypes in order to become fully integrated.

We generally all naturally identify with one archetype over the others. However, we must develop our skills in all archetypal areas.

When the pupil is ready the teacher appears and both are in turn educated.

For our purposes, we will look at the Magicians ideal attributes, then the Lover's and finally the Warrior's.

Our training begins.

Chapter 2: We develop the Magician within us.

By Joseph Anthony Campbell

Accept what you cannot change; change the things you can.

Accept what you cannot change; change the things you can and ought to change and have the wisdom to know the difference between what you should and should not change.

This is adapted from 'The Serenity Prayer' by Reinhold Niebuhr.

Is there a greater lesson than acceptance?

Once we accepted we were in the Wilderness, it was then and only then that our lives began to change.

Action is a keyword too. We are now taking steps which are often long overdue.

We also learn to outlive our problems. The moment is ever-changing. Situations change. Reality shifts.

We now assess the situations in our life honestly and accurately?

Does this situation need to be changed by me?

Does this situation need to be changed at this time?

Does this situation need to be changed at all?

Accept it or change it.

The Road to the Kingdom.

Acceptance of our past decisions.

Acceptance of our past decisions is vital.

The past is an illusion. A memory that we have in the present.

Our past decisions have led us to where we are.

They serve as a reminder of that which we have done, said and felt.

You can learn from these past decisions.

There are ultimately three courses of action that you can take in any situation.

You can accept it, change it or remove yourself.

Guilt should only serve you in perhaps affecting a change in your future decisions. It only serves you, if it serves at all.

Make your amends to the person and the situation that has caused you to feel guilt.

If you cannot make your amends, accept and resolve in your heart to act differently next time.

The past is dead. Bury it. Move into the eternal present which is your rightful home.

By Joseph Anthony Campbell

Accept indifference or even contempt from others along the Road.

Accept indifference or even contempt from others along the road.

You are seeking enlightenment in an unenlightened world.

Disrespect wounds us. Slights both real and imaginary occupy and disrupt our thoughts and emotions.

Why do we use others opinions as the barometer for our own happiness? To gauge the joy we find within our very own lives.

The same others that we are powerless over.

There can be no peace for us if we do this.

No Kingdom to attain.

We do not display indifference in return.

We do not display contempt.

We all have to ultimately take responsibility for our own actions.

How another person acts is a reflection of that person, not of us.

When others doubt us!

When others doubt us!

We use an internal boundary to listen to what they say.

We do not internalise what is said.

We maintain our internal boundaries and our inner selves are protected.

We assess their comments honestly; we are neither too lenient nor too onerous upon ourselves.

If their doubt is based on fact, we make the necessary changes.

Many times previously we have struck back like a cobra or been wounded as by a knife.

In these moments we have truly believed that what they have said is true.

Without using a boundary, without assessing the information.

Much of the insanity of the world is perpetuated in this way.

However, we now have internal boundaries. We are developing the internal armour required for our journey.

By Joseph Anthony Campbell

At times we act despite a lack of faith.

At times we act despite a lack of faith.

This is a challenge we will face as we journey upon this Road.

At times we lose faith in ourselves; it will return if we are patient, persistent and stay on the Road.

There are times when we must move on ahead despite discouragement; despite feelings of unworthiness.

The Wilderness is behind us and now we are learning how to realise the Kingdom.

We are searching for a goal that only we can see; only we can feel. At times it feels like a mirage, an illusion, even to ourselves.

We take this step now, the only step we ever really take and we move forward.

We move forward now and then unbeknownst to us we find that our faith has returned.

As Lou Holtz, the legendary American football coach said "When all is said and done, more is said than done".

We know that nothing that is worth having is achieved easily.

We begin to doubt our doubts rather than our faith.

Denying temptation.

Denying temptation.
    Succumbing to temptation has previously led us to the Wilderness.
    It is our guilt that kept us there.
    Temptation is a trial that all human beings face.
    Lust of the eyes. Lust of the flesh. The lust for power.
    All around us this temptation abounds.
    We have made resolutions; we have felt confident in our abilities to resist temptation or to indulge once more.
    We have succumbed and drowned in our guilt.
    We have left the Wilderness, we are changed beings.
    The Kingdom is within.
    We hand over responsibility to a Power that is greater than ourselves.
    And when we stumble, we get back up.
    Without guilt, without shame.
    For we are loved.

By Joseph Anthony Campbell

Accepting responsibility for yourself and for others.

Accepting responsibility for yourself and for others is the next stage upon our journey.

We are beginning to feel whole.

We have made a beginning.

We remember that the Wilderness did not demand of us that we take responsibility for ourselves.

We found a fleeting comfort in this fact.

It was the illusion of death masquerading as life.

Our personal power lies in taking responsibility for our own lives.

A sense of completeness, our emerging wholeness stems from this.

We take responsibility for our health, our wealth and our relationships. We accept responsibility for what we can control in these areas and accept what we cannot.

We then teach others how to do the same.

But first we take responsibility for ourselves. For you cannot transmit something to others that you do not already have yourself.

We tell the truth despite the consequences we may incur.

We tell the truth despite the consequences we may incur.

We tell the truth about ourselves at all times.

Yes, we have lied. We have embellished.

We may also lie again, embellish again.

But we can admit that we have lied, that we have embellished, in the past, in the present, in the future.

The truth is objective. The truth is reality. The truth was a stranger whilst we were in the Wilderness.

If there is an integrity in our agreements with others. If we are dependable and follow what Jesus said to, "let your...'Yes' be 'Yes,' and 'No,' 'No.'"[3] When we do this not to appear honest but to be honest, we are in alignment with the Kingdom.

We are not in alignment with the world.

However, it was living in the world that sent us to the Wilderness.

To the very jaws of death.

---

[3] Matt 5:37 (New Revised Standard Version)

By Joseph Anthony Campbell

Help from others may come from those you have helped previously.

Help from others may come from those you have helped previously.
 We each leave a trail. We each leave more than one.
 A trail that touches many lives for the better.
 A trail of destruction.
 The Road to the Kingdom is part of the Universal Good that exists in this world.
 There is a law summed up by Sir Isaac Newton: "To every action there is always opposed an equal reaction."[4]
 It bears a fitting resemblance to Karmic law.
 What reactions are we creating by our actions?
 As we live in line with the Good that exists in this Universe, we align ourselves with the beneficence that may come from others.
 From those we have previously helped.
 One day it may save our lives.

---

[4] **Newton, Isaac.** *Laws of Motion,* III

We learn from and honour those who have attained the Kingdom.

We learn from and honour those who have attained the Kingdom.
    Thankfully there are others who have journeyed upon this Road before us.
    Some are still with us; others have finished their time upon this earth.
    Honouring others is an important spiritual practice.
    To know that we are not alone and that there are other seekers who have attained the Kingdom restores and renews us.
    It fills us with hope.
    There are words that have been left behind, stories to be heard and images to grasp.
    We learn as we emerge upon the Road.
    We become a human being, on the path to fully realising the potential within our humanity.
    We strive to live in the only moment we ever really have.
    This one.

By Joseph Anthony Campbell

Letting people go.

Letting people go.

The Old Testament prophet Solomon said,

"For everything there is a season... a time to be born and a time to die."[5]

In our lives there are times and seasons.

There are times when we must make changes.

There are times when changes are forced upon us.

Everything changes and ultimately everything appears to end.

We must release others when it is time.

We must release our grip upon others when they need to be free. Allow them to be free. Love never forces itself upon others.

From some people we have been separated by the veil of death.

But there are realities beyond the reality we perceive.

Is anything ever really lost? Does anything ever really end?

---

[5] Ecclesiastes 3:2 (New Revised Standard Edition)

There is always hope!

There is always hope!

The present circumstances that we find ourselves in are not definitive.

The moment will change; become another moment.

Can you see beyond your present vista?

Can you see a reality beyond that which you experience?

Our future is changed by our present.

Our future will ultimately always be our present.

Hopelessness is an illusion.

It may have felt that the walls were closing in, that our breath was becoming severely restricted.

But it was not the end.

We have left the Wilderness and now we are preparing to take the Road to the Kingdom.

Our hope is becoming a reality.

By Joseph Anthony Campbell

Trust, Hope and Persevere.

Trust, hope and persevere.

    We are learning to trust others but ultimately, we must trust ourselves.

    A liar never trusts another and a person who trusts others may be considered naive.

    We can look at others objectively, if we trust ourselves.

    We can assess their intentions honestly and ultimately learn to trust those who are worthy of being trusted.

    Our hope has become a reality. However, our hope is actually found in the present moment. From the present we can affect our lives.

    The present is the window of opportunity from which we work and affect our lives.

    Our ultimately reality is always now. It is from the here and now that we find both trust and hope.

    It is from here that we persevere upon our journey.

    Moving towards our destination by continually honouring the present.

We concentrate on our efforts rather than the outcome.

We concentrate on our efforts rather than the outcome.

A vehicle often journeys upon a road for hundreds of miles in the pitch black dark and fog.

The driver can only see from the light that emits but a few metres in the distance.

Yet the driver is able to arrive safely at their destination.

This is similar to what the prophet David said: "Your word is a lamp to guide my feet and a light for my path." [6]

We do our very best, we concentrate on our efforts.

We are powerless over the outcome.

We do not focus on the outcome.

We focus only on that which we can control.

What do you have control over?

Focus on this and only this and let the outcome be what it must.

---

[6] Psalm 119:105 (New Living Translation)

By Joseph Anthony Campbell

The average person lives for approximately 28000 days.

The average person lives for approximately 28000 days. This is under 77 years.

Many people are surprised when they hear this, believing that they had hundreds of thousands of days, even millions of days of life to live.

Also, let us be clear, you do not have 28,000 days left. Your number is certainly less than this. It may be much less.

Also, there is no guarantee that you will reach 76 years of age; billions upon this Earth right now will not do so.

Approximately 151,600 people die on this Earth each day. 6,316 people die each hour. Almost two people die every second of every day. Four births also take place within every second of every day.

Your prognosis has been set. From moments to tens of years.

You do not need to have a prognosis for a terminal disease in order to start living. Everything ends on this physical plane. Enjoy now! Live now! Wake up!

Those who say the Kingdom cannot be achieved are interrupting those who are achieving it.

Those who say the Kingdom cannot be achieved are interrupting those who are achieving it.

Bronnie Ware states in her book 'The Top Five Regrets of the Dying'[7] that the top five regrets are:

1) I wish I'd had the courage to live a life true to myself, not the life others expected of me.
2) I wish I hadn't worked so hard
3) I wish I'd had the courage to express my feelings.
4) I wish I had stayed in touch with my friends.
5) I wish that I had let myself be happier.

The Kingdom is within, it is who you are.

The Kingdom requires that you make a concrete choice to find it and this involves expressing yourself fully.

This deepens your relationships and allows you to radiate joy.

The Kingdom does not involve regret.

It is not an illusion.

You are in the process of achieving it.

The first part of our training is over.

---

[7] Ware, Bronnie. *'The Top Five Regrets of the Dying'* (Balboa Press 2011.)

By Joseph Anthony Campbell

Chapter 3: We develop the Lover within us.

Trust in Love.

Trust in Love.
    Is there anything greater than love?
    Also, is there anything more misunderstood than the concept of love.
    Love is not mingled with obsession or intense longing.
    Love and hate are not opposites.
    True love has no opposite.
    Love is eternal.
    We must once again trust in love.
    When we were in the Wilderness we did not believe in love and we did not trust it.
    For love is oneness and wholeness.
    Love is complete.
    To know a Love Divine. To know it within.
    No force can stand against Love.
    Our choice is to trust in it.
    To make it the foundation from which we live our lives.

By Joseph Anthony Campbell

Although love is undeniably a feeling it is ultimately a choice.

Although love is undeniably a feeling it is ultimately a choice.

It is not to be confused with passion or lust as these feelings by their very nature, ebb and flow.

In order to love we must choose to love others. We must commit to love. To loving ourselves and others.

Love can be experienced and felt. We must choose to live our lives from it.

To act with love in our relationships. To act with love in our working lives.

To be more precise, we allow love to act through us, in our relationships and to flow outwards into the world.

The word 'love' is merely a signpost, similar to the word 'God' and often loaded with assumptions, misperceptions and misconceptions.

Love is greater than anything we can conceive of mentally.

It exists in the realm of feeling, not of thought.

It is beyond thought, beyond words and even beyond reality.

It transcends all!

We are to love one another.

We are to love one another.

Jesus stated at the Last Supper "A new commandment I give to you, that you love one another: just as I have loved you, you also are to love one another." (John 13:34: NRSV)

We are severely limited in our understanding by our one word for 'love' in the English language.

The Ancient Greeks had six definitions for love; which restricts us slightly less.

For love in its totality is beyond our understanding; beyond the intellectual mind.

Eros was used by the ancient Greeks to describe romantic love.

Ludus was used to describe playful love.

Philautia was used to describe the love of oneself.

Pragma was used to describe a longstanding love.

Philia was used to describe brotherly love.

Agape was used to describe the love for all humankind.

Agape is the love that will change the world.

It is the love of the Kingdom.

By Joseph Anthony Campbell

Love is inexhaustible.

Love is inexhaustible.

Have you experienced a romantic love for another that superseded the love you have for yourself?

If you have not found yourself, how can you find yourself within another?

It is true that love is the answer but that lust asks many questions.

We are to stay true to love despite temptation.

Despite the temptations we feel within.

No person can cure our loneliness, for loneliness comes from a sickness within.

From the Wilderness.

From being outside the Kingdom.

From being outside of our very own selves.

The physical act of love is the closest you can ever be to another human being.

We are to reflect the divine light of love. We are not to block ourselves or another from that light.

Saying goodbye to those we love.

Saying goodbye to those we love is painful.

We may not know if we will see them again.

We may have to leave without knowing if we will return.

We may know that our time with them is over.

The Road to the Kingdom involves journeying alone.

Ultimately it is a journey that we undertake alone.

Our aim is to return enriched and we surely will if we take the Road until its completion.

Then we can share our rewards with those we love.

Then we will know that our journey was for the good of all humankind, all creation.

As we contemplate taking our first steps, we become nervous.

However, we remember that we have emerged from the Wilderness and that we are building ourselves from our very foundations.

In the distance we can see the dim slopes of the Road we must travel.

The Road we must travel alone.

By Joseph Anthony Campbell

Concern for those we love above ourselves.

Concern for those we love above ourselves is necessary upon this Road.

This journey involves self-sacrifice. Sacrificing for those we love through doing what is right.

We are to do what is right for those we love, despite our personal desires.

We imprint this truth upon our hearts and minds.

The lessons we learn now will be our manual as we emerge upon the Road to the Kingdom.

They are the truths we need to sustain us and guide us as we prepare for our journey.

Remember, Philautia was once used to describe the love of oneself. It is the love that best describes the state of humankind at this present time.

We are transcending this paradigm, this way of thinking and being.

We are not alone; some are already putting those they love before themselves.

We are to join them.

We have an appreciation of the feminine and masculine in our lives.

We have an appreciation of the feminine and masculine in our lives.

Whether you are a man or woman, the opposite energy polarity is a friendly energy.

On the level of our outer selves we each need the other to be complete in our humanity.

We must not let the wounds we felt we received from our Father or substitute Fathers (real and imaginary) affect our relationships with men.

We must not let the wounds we felt we received from our Mother or substitute Mother's (real and imaginary) affect our relationships with women.

People will bask in the shade provided by those on The Road to the Kingdom.

We defend others from the elements and dangers of the world through sharing our wisdom.

We protect and guard those we love in our lives. They are an inspiration to us.

This leads to us having appropriate and worthwhile relationships with both men and women.

By Joseph Anthony Campbell

Provide children with love and safety.

Provide children with love and safety.

This includes your own children and those that you have the privilege to have in your life.

Children are near to the Kingdom.

Most children have not yet experienced the Wilderness.

Children are more present than most adults, more within the beauty of this moment.

However, they need us to provide them with love and with safety.

Our needs are to be superseded by the child's.

I know that many of us did not experience this. But we can provide it.

We can be the Father figure or Mother figure that we never had. The Father or Mother that we were looking for all our lives is ourselves.

Play with the children in your life, share in their joy. Devote your undivided attention to them.

Give love and safety; let them reflect the love they receive to others. The Love that is largely undimmed within them.

Be the light that renews.

Be the light that renews. The light that replenishes.
 This in turn helps others to shine.
 We are renewing the light within us.
 When we were in the Wilderness, we thought that the light within ourselves had been snuffed out completely.
 Yet it flickered in the darkness.
 At times, we were blocked from the light, creating ever increasing shadows.
 Ever decreasing circles of light.
 In the Wilderness, however, we could detect a dim spark in the distance.
 The light within never went out.
 The light without never went out.
 The light grows.
 In You it grows.
 In You it will be renewed.
 Others will be drawn to your flame.
 The light within you will renew the light within others.

By Joseph Anthony Campbell

> *There is nothing on Earth that we can relate to more fundamentally than another human being.*

There is nothing on Earth that we can relate to more fundamentally than another human being.

    Another human being reflects the essence of who we are back to ourselves.

    They share our emotions; they experience love and loss, pain and joy.

    They too have a mind that works against them. They too have a Spirit that they fully encapsulate.

    Can we not have compassion for this fully?

    Can we not understand their plight from the very depths of our Being?

    We are most afraid of other human beings. Of that which is most like us.

    We know that humanity can be corrupted, that we may have to stand against others actions or intentions.

    But we never lose our empathy, our sympathy, our humanness.

    We never block another human being from reaching for the light, from escaping their own Wilderness.

Be quick to forgive.

Be quick to forgive.

Forgive all who are genuinely sorry.

Resentment eats away at our souls. We suffer when we hold onto guilt, hold onto resentment.

We would not continue to hold on to barbed wire as our hands bleed profusely.

Do not hold on to anger, resentment and non-forgiveness.

Do not shorten the quantity of the days of your life and the quality of them also.

We wish to be forgiven.

We must assess our resentments and our own part in these resentments accurately.

First, we forgive others fully then ourselves.

To forgive does not mean that we condone the actions that were done against us or the actions that we ourselves have done.

Ultimately, we forgive and honour those alive, dying and dead.

For this, too, is what we would wish to be done by others for ourselves.

By Joseph Anthony Campbell

We have an affinity with animals and nature.

We have an affinity with animals and nature.

The enlightened person is in touch with the oneness of all that is perceived.

Have you ever noticed how animals are at one with the present moment? They are fully in the now.

Those who are on "The Road to the Kingdom" attract animals towards them, dogs, cats, horses; it is as though they sense the purity of your journey. The alignment of your soul with the Universe.

A dog offers unconditional love, can you do that?

Can you sit and look at a river and appreciate its beauty?

Have you ever really looked at a flower?

I mean truly looked at it, felt the connection between you and it?

Have you ever had your breath taken away by a view, a tree or a blossoming orchard?

What is it in us that identifies so strongly?

Do you know you have a soul?

We are grateful.

We are grateful.

We have gratitude for all that is. This is the way of the Kingdom.

We appreciate that we are alive and give thanks for this. We notice the beauty all around us.

We have another day of life and our lives are not limitless. We should be grateful for this.

Do you have love in your life? Even if you feel you do not, how much love do you have to give?

Love is everywhere. Love is limitless and inexhaustible.

It takes no money to give love, simply a choice, a choice to act with love, to let love act through you.

Love was a distant dream that we believed to be illusory as we languished in the Wilderness.

As we develop our gratitude for all that we experience and have experienced. All that we perceive and have perceived. We know that love is not an illusion.

It is not even a simple piece of bliss that occasionally lightens the gloom of our everyday lives.

It is our natural state. It is our natural home.

By Joseph Anthony Campbell

We are kind to others.

We are kind to others.

One day your life will end. What will you be remembered for?

Did you spare the feelings of others? Did you seek to understand others viewpoints?

Were you grateful? Did you love all those around you?

Were you kind?

If you were kind to others you will be remembered fondly. However, being kind is a reward in and of itself.

We are now discovering as we emerge from the Wilderness, the full extent of our empathy and compassion for other humans.

We know we cannot transmit something that we do not have.

We must be kind to ourselves and we are now developing the ability to be kind to others.

We know that kindness to others never fails and therefore we now provide kindness at each and every opportunity that arises. We do this not for approval but because it is the right thing to do.

Wishing joy for others.

Wishing joy for others.

To wish joy upon others is to confer blessings upon another and to be pleased for their good fortune.

We are actually blessing ourselves as we bless others.

If those around us are having good fortune then this will surely lead to ourselves experiencing this. A high tide raises all ships.

However, we can also simply wish joy for others so that they themselves will experience joy and we spare no thought for ourselves as we do this.

We are learning to think of others.

We are sharing in others joy.

If others are in the Wilderness and do not have joy, we still hope and pray that they receive it.

It is our sincere wish that they too are able to leave the Wilderness.

To leave the pain, the pain of the Wilderness.

A pain that we have known intimately.

By Joseph Anthony Campbell

We aim to help those who have been damaged by the past.

We aim to help those who have been damaged by the past.

We now appreciate the pain that others have suffered. We now have empathy and compassion for them.

We are beginning to free ourselves from the pain of the past.

To free ourselves from damage that we thought may be irrevocable.

We are learning that the pain of the past can be transformed by the present.

We work with others. We work on allowing them to free themselves from the damage of the past.

They are our brothers and sisters. There is no real distance between us. All the distance that we perceive is merely an illusion.

Do you know that there are atoms within our body that were forged by stars? We are made of stars, we are stardust. Remember this as you look into the night sky.

We apply our worldly thinking to phenomena that is beyond that which we can ever truly comprehend.

> *People are not to be used for the love of money; money is to be used to love people.*

People are not to be used for the love of money; money is to be used to love people.

We have all suffered from greed that infects our soul. We have all been infected from within.

Some of us have experienced our own darkness through the reflection of our greed for money.

Through our desire for it. Or the desire of the world to obtain it from us and our desire to obtain it from the world.

In this current era, money has replaced the spiritual, replaced the sacred.

We are each trapped in a world that was devised before we were born and presented money as an idol unto us. A literal golden idol to be worshipped.

Money is a necessity in our world. However, money is not our master, it is our servant. It can serve to love people. Therefore, be in the flow of having and giving.

But do not make an idol of it as people are infinitely more important. Our souls are more important.

The Kingdom is beyond it. Beyond anything it can purchase. Beyond anything it represents.

By Joseph Anthony Campbell

> *The ability to love and nurture began with the mother's warmth, the mother's love.*

The ability to love and nurture began with the mother's warmth, the mother's love.

Through this love we can experience love and attain the power to love others.

For many of us, we were able to experience this directly from our mothers, from our grandmothers or the substitute mothers that were placed in our lives.

Some of us feel we did not experience this. There are many of us also who experienced this love but we were too self-obsessed to see it. There are those of us also who do not feel worthy of love.

However, the feminine life principle is all around us. Within the principles of creation itself.

A human being will not survive past the first few weeks of their life without care. Unlike some animals we cannot fend for ourselves for many years after we are born.

We are alive. We have been cared for.

We have been and are loved and cared for.

Now go and love and care for others.

We minister to the sick.

We minister to the sick.

There are different types of sickness. Physical, mental and emotional.

There is also a spiritual sickness, of which all of us have suffered to some extent.

When we were in the Wilderness we were in a spiritual desert. Now, at last, we have found an oasis as we emerge from the Wilderness. It has proven itself to not be a mirage.

We are preparing for the Road to the Kingdom. The Kingdom is the source of all spiritual life. Of this oasis.

Now we have compassion and aim to provide comfort to those who mourn and to alleviate their pain.

We stand alongside those who are watching their loved ones leave this earth.

We have compassion and empathy for those who face tragedy. We stand shoulder to shoulder with those who feel alone.

They are not alone, for we are with them and we provide solace to those who feel that they are truly alone.

We do this whenever our paths cross with theirs.

By Joseph Anthony Campbell

We help others even when we are in need.

We help others even when we are in need.

This is the act of a truly heroic person.

As we suffer, we alleviate another's suffering.

If it is in our power to act then we do so.

We are beginning to sense through our emergence from the Wilderness and learning about the skills of the true Magician and of the person who truly loves, something beyond ourselves.

Of consequences we affect that are too far reaching for our minds to comprehend.

We are aware of something much greater than ourselves.

It is this awareness that is freeing us. Freeing us from the burden of ourselves, our thoughts, emotions, fears and unrealistic expectations.

We may be in need but still we help others.

For we are now becoming the recipients of that which we have always truly needed.

We acknowledge and honour those who are often overlooked.

We acknowledge and honour those who are often overlooked.

We are no longer seeking praise for ourselves. Our honour is returning.

There are many in this world that are considered useless, if they do not earn a certain amount of money or have a certain physical appearance.

We know that the importance and value placed upon money and our physical appearance is ultimately an illusion.

At some point we will all have to give these aspects of ourselves up fully. They will dissolve.

In this world they are held in the highest esteem.

Those who lack these attributes are often overlooked. However, those who worship at the altar of money and of physical beauty experience great pain.

We acknowledge all people including those who are overlooked and we do not refrain from stating clearly that which is real and that which is simply an illusion.

The Road to the Kingdom is not the road towards the world.

It runs counter to it.

It runs within.

By Joseph Anthony Campbell

We have a gentle and firm way.

We have a gentle and firm way.
    Be both gentle and meek.
    'Meek' originally meant 'strength under control'.
    What could be more useful than great strength that is under control?
    Strength that is to be used only when necessary.
    We do not refrain from telling the truth. We can state the truth clearly and calmly to others.
    Yet we remain fluid.
    As Lao Tzu stated,
    "Water is the softest thing, yet it can penetrate mountains and earth".[8]
    This is a gentle and firm way. Water is a living thing, it gives our very bodies life, yet it can move mountains.
    Our aim is to make allies of others. We want to be able to engage with others. We want to be approachable and inviting.
    For every human being is an integral part of the divine puzzle.
    Each and every one of us is worth more than we could ever conceive.

---

[8] Tzu, Lao: *Tao Te Ching*

We are becoming humble.

We are becoming humble.

Being humble does not mean thinking less of yourself, it means thinking of yourself less.

We have acquired wisdom and aptitudes in our training. When we journey upon the Road others may witness our actions and ask us how we have acquired the skills and the knowledge that we have now.

They may also hear of our skills and aptitude through others.

However, we do not boast about our own achievements and we are not affecting mock humility.

Others may discover our achievements through our actions or through the words of another or they may not.

It is of no concern.

We are not on the Road for personal gain. Our gains are for all men and women and even when they are fully realised we will remain humble.

We experience life in every breath not through the praise of others.

By Joseph Anthony Campbell

We have an appreciation for the beauty of our existence.

We have an appreciation for the beauty of our existence.

We live on land that is surrounded by water. The water makes up over two thirds of the Earth. Our bodies too are comprised of over two thirds of water.

The Earth itself is moving at 1000 miles an hour which we do not feel because we ourselves are moving at exactly the same rate as part of the Earth's contents.

Our planet is the third planet from the Sun within the Solar System. A Sun that is 93 million miles away and our solar system has 9 planets.

The speed of light is 193,000 miles per second.

Travelling at the speed of light it takes 28,000 light years to reach 'Galactic Central Point'.

Our Galaxy is one of an infinite number of Galaxies.

We are part of a great mystery. Everything is moving. There is infinite distance around us.

We are part of an inconceivable canvas of creation. We are both integral and infinitely minute within the Universe.

This beauty is limitless and boundless.

The Road to the Kingdom.

We have an appreciation of History and our ancestors.

We have an appreciation of History and our ancestors.
    We have looked at the cosmos before us and now we look at where we are.
    We are on this Earth and have the time we are given to live our lives upon it.
    We appreciate that others have asked the same questions we are now asking.
    That others have journeyed upon the Road to the Kingdom.
    We have an appreciation for our ancestors who struggled too with the human condition.
    Through our ancestors we have been brought to this exact point. Through them the foundations have been set.
    We have a new-found respect for them and honour their lives.

By Joseph Anthony Campbell

We honour other cultures.

We honour other cultures.

In terms of the Universe we realise how truly minute our planet is. How bound we are to it.

We have learnt that in terms of the Universe, the Earth's population is just a tiny tribe.

This knowledge enables us to honour, respect and appreciate all the cultures upon our Earth.

To honour, appreciate and respect all that other cultures hold dear.

We have learnt how alike we are to another human being.

We are all human.

We learn from other cultures.

We appreciate their customs.

We are always respectful.

We are always discerning and open-minded.

Ultimately, we embrace our common humanity.

We speak well of others.

We speak well of others.
    We know that the tongue can be deadlier than any weapon.
    We do not deal in lies, we deal with the truth.
    We reflect the truth despite the fact that our truth may be twisted into a lie.
    Rudyard Kipling states this best,
    "If you can bear to hear the truth you've spoken. Twisted by knaves to make a trap for fools." [9]
    It is one of Kipling's conditions that he presents to his son on becoming a man.
    We also honour those who have authority.
    Often others have authority because they have a special ability in their area, a special understanding.
    This is not always the case but we always assume the best of people when we first meet them.
    We also honour others achievements. We are pleased for them and we are happy to speak favourably of what they have achieved.

---

[9] Kipling, Rudyard. *If* POETRY FOUNDATION

By Joseph Anthony Campbell

Love and tolerance.

Love and tolerance of others is our code.

This is the truth that we have learned as we conclude the lessons that develop the Lover within us.

Through Love and tolerance, we are also able to express ourselves fully. Love and tolerance will be vital tools for us when we travel along The Road to the Kingdom.

Love is a concept that has frequently been misunderstood. We now feel clearer on what it truly means to love. For love goes hand in hand with tolerance.

We will encounter people with different views, different intentions upon this Road. This is where tolerance will prove vital.

But we must also decide what is tolerable and what is not.

The time of the Warrior is upon us.

Our Way is the Way of the Peaceful Warrior.

We have learnt of peace. Now we must learn how to maintain and transmit this peace in the arena of war.

Chapter 4: We develop the Warrior within us.

By Joseph Anthony Campbell

Do not stand down. Do not stand aside. Do not stand against. Stand up!

Do not stand down. Do not stand aside. Do not stand against. Stand up!

We now must develop the Warrior within.

This time of the Warrior is the final part of our training.

The Warrior is the part of us that can execute the clean swipe of the sword when absolutely necessary.

The part of us that can construct the boundaries that will be needed before we face our final battle. The battle to realise the Kingdom.

We do not stand down when the time for action comes.

We do not stand aside when our conscience dictates that we must speak up.

We do not stand against, for we are not confrontational; we are peaceful Warriors, fighting only when necessary for the betterment of all humankind.

It is only when we must that we stand up. To defend the 'Truth' and the 'Good' that still exists in this world.

We now reflect and respond rather than react.

We now reflect and respond rather than react to life's challenges.
    We do not react to others' anger.
    We reflect upon it.
    Their anger may even be directed at us unfairly.
    We can respond without reacting.
    We can say no without being angry.
    We can state that their anger is being directed at us unfairly in a calm and clear way.
    This is counter intuitive to the behaviour of our 'modern' world.
    We are not diminished by the unfair comments of others.
    We are peaceful Warriors.
    Peaceful warriors who have glimpsed a great reality.
    The reality that the resistance of others provides us with greater inner strength.

By Joseph Anthony Campbell

Life is 10% what happens to you and 90% how you respond to it.

"Life is 10% what happens to you and 90% how you respond to it". Lou Holtz the legendary American football coach said this.

    Life is relentless. It is always happening. It always already is. Here and now.

    There are many events that happen to us.

    How we react to what happens to us is decisive in determining the quality of the life that we live.

    We can make what has happened (or we think has happened) infinitely worse than the event itself (which may or may not be imaginary).

    We can perform actions that deepen our problem significantly.

    This creates a cycle of ever increasing and difficult events for us to face before it becomes how we perceive our very life itself.

    Or we can react calmly, discern the actual facts, face the facts directly and then either take action if necessary, accept the situation or remove ourselves from it.

    We can stop the rot. Now.

Offering our hand even if it may be refused.

Offering our hand even if it may be refused is the action of an enlightened person.

We are peaceful Warriors and our aim is to make allies of others.

There is a boldness in risking rejection and assuming the best of people. In encouraging others.

There is no guarantee that your smile will be returned and that your hand will be clasped warmly.

There is no guarantee that you will in turn be encouraged.

It is of no concern.

We may face a glare of hatred, our hand may be spat upon, and we may be actively discouraged.

We do not derive our worth from others. We can walk away. We can politely but clearly disagree.

However, we may also be a wellspring of kindness that changes and transforms another person's life by our actions.

The potential risk is well worth the potential reward.

By Joseph Anthony Campbell

The Road to the Kingdom involves courage, benevolence and decisiveness.

The Road to the Kingdom involves courage, benevolence and decisiveness.

We must be strong, courageous, stoic, beneficent, modest and independent.

A protector and a provider on all levels.

A Warrior.

Ultimately, we have made a decision to love others.

We are to be benevolent to others as we have developed a love for them.

We have had some respite from the Wilderness but we are beginning to now realise that we must develop the courage that is deep within us.

This, too, first begins with a decision.

The decision to be a fully realised human being and to realise our potential in each and every moment.

In order to achieve this, we have to develop the courage to face our deepest fears.

To face them is to emerge victorious. Whatever the outcome.

Patience and discipline.

Patience and discipline are part of the Warrior's code.

As we languished in the Wilderness, we may have believed that we were patient.

But secretly we perhaps believed that things would simply change imminently without any effort on our part.

We expected it to end in days and instead we languished for years; too many years.

Now we can direct the years ahead whilst fully honouring the step we are taking.

Every moment of our training is necessary for the Road ahead.

To be in a full state of readiness we must have discipline and combine this with the patience to allow our training to come to fruition.

When full preparation meets the perfect opportunity, the result is inevitability.

We are now at the point of no return as the Wilderness' shadow recedes into the distance.

By Joseph Anthony Campbell

Courage determines the quality of your life.

Courage determines the quality of your life.

    We must find once again the courage that is within. This began when we found the courage to leave our Wilderness.

    In the deepest resources of our innermost selves lies the courage that we need. Courage is like a muscle, we must train it, ensuring it is there when we most need it.

    To act with courage is a decision. We display the courage to act even when we are deeply afraid of what we have to face.

    Consequences will befall us due to our acts of courage. However, we know that the consequences worsen when we do not take action.

    The world lacks courage. Throughout the world there are those who cry out for those brave men and women who would display the courageousness to help.

    There is plenty of work to do.

    Courage is needed to rescue ourselves.

    Courage is needed to rescue others.

    Courage is needed to rescue the world.

    We have decided that we are those gallant few who will dare to rescue ourselves, others and ultimately the world.

    To the utmost of our ability!

The Hunt.

The hunt.

Now we have the earth as our teacher.

We are preparing the Warrior within us. With courage we develop our endurance.

We learn to hunt, to track, to forage and ultimately to provide for ourselves. We are becoming independent and strong.

We must also defend ourselves against the elements.

We become one with the cold, the swirling winds and the ever-changing weather.

Testing ourselves against the elements we develop our internal and external strength.

We move from crawling to walking. Up ahead lies a place where we must run.

We are learning what it will take to journey upon The Road to the Kingdom.

Knowing this, we welcome all challenges, for they develop our strength. They provide us with the character needed to survive the Road.

By Joseph Anthony Campbell

We keep our sword sharp.

We keep our sword sharp.

The Semiotics of symbols such as a metaphorical 'sword' symbol is important.

For our 'sword' may be our words, how we devote our time and the actions that we take. Our 'sword' is the talent and gifts that we inherently possess.

Whatever our sword is, whatever weapon we use most effectively, this is the weapon we use.

This is the sword which promotes peace and love throughout a broken world.

Whatever our sword is, we harness its power.

We sharpen it against the stone of our personal and collective challenges.

We will find that the challenges that we face will grow.

Our sword must become increasingly sharp in order to meet these challenges head-on.

In time, the sword becomes an extension of ourselves; of our Souls.

This is a necessity, as each person has an ultimate battle that they must undertake.

We endure when we must in order to survive.

We endure when we must in order to survive.

At times, we will experience lack.

This can remind us of the Wilderness.

However, now we are doing the best we can with what we have.

In the Wilderness we languished and backslid towards darkness and death.

Now, instead, we are laying solid foundations, built from our own hands.

Foundations that will last.

Before what we are building within comes to fruition, we will experience doubt.

We will, at times, struggle for survival.

Our food may be meagre and our pack light, as we develop the skills of a Warrior.

However, we know that our redemption is at hand. We can and will survive on these meagre rations, with barely the clothes on our back.

We will endure what is necessary to survive when we must.

For the Road is our destiny and we cannot and will not turn back.

By Joseph Anthony Campbell

Defeats along the Road.

Defeats along the Road.
    There will be defeats upon The Road.
    There will be defeats delivered at the hands of both ourselves and others.
    Letting ourselves down can at times be acutely painful.
    We must remind ourselves that we are doing our best.
    We must remind ourselves that we are human and that mistakes are at times inevitable.
    We do aim to learn from our defeats, to avoid their re-occurrence. We do this to the best of our ability.
    We analyse and assess what happened accurately and fairly and may even enlist the help of others we trust, to explain where they feel we went wrong.
    After this time of reflection, we rectify the situation if we can. Then we move forward.
    We gain fresh insight into our weaknesses, into which defeats are self-inflicted and which are not.
    We move forward. With new knowledge, we press ahead.

Do not doubt your faith; doubt your doubt.

Do not doubt your faith; doubt your doubt.

There will be times when we are plagued with doubt. When we believe that we cannot succeed.

We will ask ourselves "Who are we that we should realise the Kingdom?" We may even doubt the very existence of such a place.

We may believe we are fighting odds against us that are too great. We may even find others who will agree with our negative predictions.

This is in fact a vital part of the process we are undertaking. We must accept and acknowledge our doubts and bring them into the light, as in the dark they gain power.

We realise through honest reflection that the Wilderness was once our home.

We realise that it is enough simply to create distance from ourselves and that place. We may not know where we are headed but we know where we have been.

Therefore, we act despite self-doubt and despite no assurance of success.

Then, when we feel doubt and sadness, we stop feeling this way and feel and express our awesomeness instead.

By Joseph Anthony Campbell

Protecting with our very lives.

Protecting with our very lives.

As we embrace our doubts openly, a new strength emerges within us.

We feel a new nobility; a new strength being borne by what we perceived was our weakness.

Doubt is a part of the human condition. There can be no certainty for us and this gives us a new faith.

We are beginning to experience the seeds of greatness within ourselves. Fleetingly at first but they are there.

As long as we remain honest with ourselves and others, this honesty will act as water for the seeds of greatness within.

We are beginning to entertain what was once a curious notion. That we would defend the good of this world with our lives.

We are restoring our own honour. We are building the readiness we need to fight the good fight.

To dedicate our lives in service to and for the protection of; all that is good in this world.

Knowing *when* to take action.

Knowing *when* to take action.

There are times when we must take action and there are times when we must refrain from doing so.

We each have particular talents, through honest self-assessment we find out what they are.

There are times when we are not the right answer to a person's particular challenge.

There are situations where our presence may even worsen the problem that is being faced.

We may also find at times that we are powerless to help another. That they are set upon their own path to destruction.

When we know we cannot help, we regretfully have to stand aside.

We know there will be other battles where we will be of vital importance.

We, too, must maintain our strength for the battles that lie ahead.

For we have learnt a painful truth.

As with ourselves, we are only able to help others if they truly want to be helped.

By Joseph Anthony Campbell

Embracing the moment for leadership.

Embracing the moment for leadership without hesitation is vital for a Warrior.

Therefore, we volunteer for noble duties.

Concentrating our energies on all that is good and honourable in this world, we take the moment that arises when we must provide direction and a noble purpose, without hesitation.

We have cultivated and harnessed our abilities throughout our training and we have been set on an inexorable path with this moment.

We must learn to recognise this moment when it arises and embrace the opportunity it presents.

We know that those we lead and those that are led are part of a single motion. That to lead others in integrity is an act of love.

We too are led by those who know more in particular areas. We both teach and continue to learn and we always honour those we lead by recognising their unique talents.

Protecting the vulnerable.

Protecting the vulnerable and protecting the quest of another are duties undertaken by the Warrior.

We alert others to potential pitfalls and dangers.

We do not keep our knowledge to ourselves. We are to transmit what we have learnt to others.

There will be times too when our own journey, our own quest, will be subservient to that of another.

This develops a Warriors strength and their noble ideal of service for others.

The inner journey that we are on is fully honoured when we protect the quest of another. When we protect the vulnerable, those who have no one to protect them, we are travelling upon the Road to the Kingdom.

Unfortunately, we will witness others succumb to darkness fully, to the Wilderness and beyond.

We do our best to prevent this but we also learn to recognise when we are powerless.

We ourselves, will not be enveloped by this darkness. Our noble actions act as a sure defence against it.

By Joseph Anthony Campbell

Maintaining hope, no matter what we are facing.

Maintaining hope, no matter what we are facing. We are both brave and loyal and stand side by side with those in peril.

We encourage others in their times of dire need.

We place our hands upon others shoulders, make direct eye contact and encourage others.

There are times when what we face will appear too overwhelming, too monstrous for us to have any hope of prevailing against.

However, this is our moment, the moment we have trained for.

No matter what and who we face, if we have no other option, we stand up.

Our hope remains and we transmit this to others. If we are to be defeated in this battle, then let it be that we gave our all. This gives permission for others to put forth their most valiant efforts also.

We will rally others to our noble cause.

We do this through transmitting our undimmed hope to them. No matter how great the opponent.

Face your fears and difficulties.

Face your fears and difficulties; the storms of life.

'The Man in the Arena' speech by Theodore Roosevelt delivered in 1910 in Paris brilliantly exemplifies this.

As Roosevelt states, ''Strive valiantly with your face marred with sweat and dust, with great devotions to a worthy cause; daring greatly.''[10]

We must always believe in ourselves when we face the inevitable storms in our life.

We believe that we will overcome.

We are soon to take the Road to the Kingdom.

We are soon to face battles upon this Road.

Persistence is key.

We make a decision to never give up whilst we have breath left.

We will face our fears, our internal and external battles.

We make a decision to be the first in and the last out when our inevitable battles arise.

---

[10] Roosevelt, Theodore: *Citizenship in a Republic* (1910)

By Joseph Anthony Campbell

Ride out and meet the enemy.

Ride out and meet the enemy.

We have decided that we will give our all upon the Road with no holding back.

We know that there will be battles to face before the ultimate and final battle for the Kingdom.

We acknowledge that our training is now over.

We acknowledge the sacrifice of others.

We acknowledge those who helped lead us from the Wilderness.

Those who taught us the necessary skills to take the Road to the Kingdom.

We honour those who have fallen upon or left the Road and we know that we all must do this at some time.

We have decided to live our lives fully.

We move inexorably onwards.

We take the Road to The Kingdom.

Chapter 5: We journey upon The Road to the Kingdom.

By Joseph Anthony Campbell

We now have the necessary understanding.

We now have the necessary understanding of what it means to be a Magician, Lover and Warrior as a man.

We reflect upon all that we have learnt.

We have developed our intelligence and wisdom through our training to develop the Magician within us.

We have developed our compassion, our empathy and our ability to love and be loved through our training to develop the Lover within us.

We have developed the courage that is required within our very souls, to enable us to face the inevitable battles that lie ahead, through our training to develop the Warrior within us.

The Wilderness appears almost unreal now. Our scars however remind us of its reality. For the wounds we obtained there still ache occasionally. But the pain is duller now, much less acute.

The time for action is upon us.

We have made a decision to take the Road.

We may not return from our journey and we know we will be forever changed even if we do.

After training, we act.

After training, we act.

The moment before a courageous act can seem lonely but we commit to giving our all. All that we have within us with no holding back.

We are ready to emerge upon the Road to the Kingdom.

This present moment contains our decision to realise the Kingdom.

Having left our place of isolation, first in the Wilderness and then as we developed the skills required for the Road ahead through our training, we can now become the person that we were born to be.

We are committed to the path.

This Road, the Road to the Kingdom is a journey that most will never undertake.

We have been willing to learn things that others will never know and we remain willing.

We remain willing to learn and to receive the rewards that we are destined for and *then* to share those rewards with others.

By Joseph Anthony Campbell

We take the Road and follow it until its final destination; the Kingdom.

We take the Road and follow it until its final destination; the Kingdom.

We embrace our destiny anew and resume the Road ahead.

This involves risk, fear and change, for our opportunity lies within the opposition that life presents to us.

We must face the difficult tasks that the Road will present unto us. We must call upon the deep recesses of courage that lie within us.

For we will be refined upon The Road and establish our independence and competence.

We have developed our abilities. We are ready to face hostile environments and people who are in direct opposition to our realisation of the Kingdom.

We are prepared to test ourselves.

To face our limitations and weaknesses.

To face the seemingly immovable.

We are restoring a broken lineage.

We are restoring a broken lineage, whereby our rightful heritage; our rightful title; our destiny as a future King or Queen of the Kingdom makes itself known.

Being known by our rightful title and heritage will be earned from the integrity of our actions.

Therefore, we have incredible integrity. We display our qualities of being both honest and having strong moral principles.

We assert and define ourselves as Kings and Queens and relate to others fully and creatively.

We are not restricted by the integrity of our actions. In fact, what some perceive as a restriction, gives us a clear focus, it clarifies our thinking which in turn clarifies the actions we must take.

There is no confusion as our actions *must* be infused with integrity.

From the dying embers of the Wilderness to the flame that has emerged since, we are now set aflame with our purpose.

Our broken lineage is being fully restored.

By Joseph Anthony Campbell

Our past does not equal our future.

Our past does not equal our future as we journey upon the Road.

We begin to fully eliminate the scar tissue of our past and to come to terms with our own personal history which has led to this path; this Road.

We drop the past, leave it and will not pick it up again and let it go.

We have our own funeral for the difficult events of our past and we refuse to dig them up again.

We become present and move forward; honouring the step we are taking now. The only step we ever really have to take in life.

Our mind is renewed, we are beginning to be reinvented and our inner selves are protected.

We develop emotional control and move through our fears as we embark upon this Road; this journey towards becoming a true human being.

We acknowledge our qualities.

We acknowledge our qualities and accept those who refuse or cannot see them.

Our qualities are within us no matter what they say.

There will be those who deny that we have changed. They deny that we are on the Road to the Kingdom.

Some will believe that they are saving us from pain. Some will believe that they are being realistic. Some may even say such things out of spite and envy, threatened by what we are becoming.

We examine ourselves to determine whether there is an element of truth to what they are saying.

If we find that there is no truth in their words, it is of no concern, as our qualities are becoming clearly apparent to us.

After we have tasted battles and succeeded, we begin to embrace our status as an heir.

We have the Kingdom inside of us.

We are simply manifesting it in the battles that we face.

We now become deeply aware that we are transcending former realities.

By Joseph Anthony Campbell

We accept the praise of mentors.

We accept the praise of mentors.

We find that mentors appear upon the Road.

When we have been on the Road for a significant amount of time, we learn to accept all praise from mentors and other people, with dignity.

We do not deflect it, nor do we feed the ego.

Yet we have learnt not to disqualify ourselves from praise. We accept compliments graciously.

We have journeyed upon the Road for a little while now.

We bear fresh scars, but unlike when we received them in the Wilderness, they are now scars of our own choosing.

For we have chosen to take the Road.

Or to be more precise the Road has chosen us.

We are becoming aware that there were only ever two opposing directions upon the Road.

One leading towards the Wilderness and the other that leads now towards the Kingdom.

Our weakness is becoming our strength.

Our weakness is becoming our strength.
    Our wounds are healing and this fills us with courage.
    For we have explored the darkest caves within ourselves.
    We have faced them unblinkingly.
    We have emerged victorious
    Daring to face the unknown.
    We have developed the strengths that once lay dormant within ourselves.
    The spark of our greatness becomes a flame!
    We now find that we are in a position of strength when formerly we languished in despair within a Wilderness that at times was of our own making.
    Yet we never forget where we came from.
    And we never cease trying to deliver others from their entrapment within the Wilderness.

By Joseph Anthony Campbell

A personal destiny has emerged.

A personal destiny has emerged upon the Road.
    The dream that was deferred is being realised
    We have learnt that there is still time!
    As long as we are breathing there is still time.
    We know we cannot be protected from our destiny.
    We know that refusal of the road is not possible.
    We must forge ahead.
    We remember that we must make the most of our time on this Road as one day we all must leave it.
    We have learnt that anxiety and anger have no place upon the Road.
    We aim to remove anxiety and anger from our innermost selves.
    In order to reduce their power as outward manifestations.
    Our mess has become our message.
    Our test our testimony.

We made a concrete decision to follow The Road to the Kingdom.

We made a concrete decision to follow The Road to the Kingdom.

We have been in the Wilderness.

We have emerged from the Wilderness.

We have developed the necessary skills as a Magician, a Lover and a Warrior and we have reflected upon our training in these areas.

We have now journeyed upon the Road for a while.

We have tasted success in some battles, defeats in others.

Yet we still remain on the Road.

Some of the battles hurt us to our very blood. Our very bones.

We are aware that an ultimate battle awaits.

We become increasingly aware that at this moment we cannot succeed in this final battle.

That without help we will be obliterated.

By Joseph Anthony Campbell

At times we experienced supernatural help.

At times we experienced supernatural help.

We catch our breath and reflect upon the supernatural help that we experienced upon the Road.

At times we have faced danger, even annihilation upon the Road.

Then, the right thought or action suddenly became known to us.

We experienced supernatural help too within the Wilderness.

Otherwise we would not have survived.

These thoughts create a crystallisation of our current purpose and dilemma.

The Final Battle looms.

Our bodies are bruised but not beaten. Yet we know in our hearts that we are not ready.

To take part in the ultimate battle within ourselves and without we must emerge upon a new chapter.

We need to fully develop our inner armour, the spiritual armour within us, before we can face this ultimate battle.

Chapter 6: We reflect upon Spiritual truths before our Final Battle.

By Joseph Anthony Campbell

We must seek out the Power that is greater than all things.

We must seek out the Power that is greater than all things.

    We must take this final step before we engage in our Final Battle.

    We know in our hearts and our souls that we must enter our sacred place; a Temple, a Mosque, a Church, any place that is sacred to us and we must seek out the Power that is greater than all things.

    The Power that made us.

    We kneel.

    We recount quietly to ourselves what we have learnt thus far on our journey.

    We enter communion with our Higher Power.

    Our head is bowed.

    We ask for the truth.

    We ask that this Source/Power/God/Being/Creator give us victory in our Final Battle.

    We delve deep into our Spirituality.

All words are mere pointers to a transcendent reality.

All words are mere pointers to a transcendent reality.

We can call this transcendent reality our Source, God, Power, Creator, Being or any other name.

The Living Reality of God in every moment of our lives is more powerful than any mental concept.

The reality of God is within us.

We explore this truth further and realise some seminal truths.

We recall times upon the Road when we happened upon the embankment of a river.

We put down our swords and our packs but for a brief moment, occasionally for longer.

We studied the river. It was in all places at all times.

We watched the sunlight fragment and dance upon the river's surface.

We heard the birds singing, and felt the aliveness of the Universe.

We felt the glory of all that is both within us and surrounds us.

By Joseph Anthony Campbell

Life is always now.

Life is always now.
It always has been, always will be and always is now.
It unfolds in one moment.
Within the moment our lives are lived and all that has been and will be and is emerges and disappears in this moment.

    We are part of the moment now.
    We must be here now!
    The Road to the Kingdom takes place now!
    This now, this quintessential constantly fleeting, momentary reality that shifts always and at all times to a new moment, a new now.
    The reality of the moment is re-configured at all moments, at all points.
    We are part of all that has been, is and will be.
    Therefore, we have made friends with the present moment.
    We have learnt upon the Road to say 'Yes' to what is.
    To whatever the moment is.
    We realise that the time is always NOW.

Accept everything as it is.

Accept everything as it is.
   Once again, we realise that acceptance is key.
   The past is gone and the future is not here yet.
   The past will always be gone and the future will never arrive, only as the present moment.
   As the now that we are always already experiencing.
   Be here now.
   We concentrate our energies upon this moment.
   We fully commit to this time of reflection. This moment.
   When the battle is to be fought, we will give ourselves fully too, to that moment.
   We experience a total trust, a total faith that everything is as it should be at this moment.
   We accept that we will desire the moment to shift to what we perceive as a more pleasing reality at times.
   By fully accepting this we begin to embrace the present moment more fully; at times we can embrace the present moment completely!

By Joseph Anthony Campbell

Non-resistance, non-judgment and non-attachment.

Non-resistance, non-judgment and non-attachment.

Upon the Road we have learnt that resistance at times brought forth greater levels of resistance.

Therefore: We became fluid like water.

We practiced non-resistance.

We realised too, that all humans acted only as they had the capacity to do at the time.

We forgave. We were clear with others but we did not judge. Judgement was the responsibility of a Power greater than ourselves.

We practiced non-judgement.

We too, had realised that all physical forms emerge and pass into the now, which will include our own.

We love people but we know that all is temporal upon this Earth.

Yet we felt that nothing real is ever truly lost.

We practiced non-attachment to physical forms.

Through these three practices we become thankful daily for our lives.

For what we already have; life.

The Road to the Kingdom is a Spiritual journey.

The Road to the Kingdom is a Spiritual journey.
    It was a truth both simple and stunningly clear to us now.
    What we were interested in was truth.
    The reality of truth.
    The question had always been, was there a Higher Power?
    A God who cared about us?
    A God who would help us upon our journey through this life?
    A God we could call upon to help ourselves and others?
    A God we could trust?
    A single unifying force both within ourselves and throughout the Universe?
    We asked in prayer and meditation for the truth.
    We know that the truth is the truth no matter what we say or believe.
    That it's objective reality can never be changed by our subjective interpretations.

By Joseph Anthony Campbell

The Road to faith is a deeply personal journey.

The Road to faith is a deeply personal journey.

This is the Road our Creator wants us to journey upon.

We can call this unifying force, our Source, God, Power, Creator, Being or any other name.

We were learning to trust in God.

We were now beginning a true relationship with our Creator.

We had faith in the reality of God.

Yes, there is darkness.

However, we have learned that the darkness does not understand four human emotions: 'Gratitude', 'Acceptance', 'Forgiveness' and 'Love'.

These emotions lead to presence in this moment.

The darkness is terrified of what you can become when you are present in the moment and will try to stop this.

We fully commit to the God of our understanding. [11]

This is vital for the continuation of our journey upon the Road to the Kingdom.

---

[11] I now refer to this Higher Power as God, which I choose to call Him but please remember that all words are mere pointers to a transcendent reality. Please feel free to substitute the word God for a Higher Power of your own understanding.

We accept that God made this Road.

We accept that God made this Road and the Kingdom.
  That God will supernaturally help us.
  We are but a trail of stardust leading to the Superstar.
  The Spirit of God is within us.
  The Grace of God surrounds us.
  Our Creator keeps our blood flowing and our body breathing.
  We have life in every breath.
  We turn to God for help, no matter what we face.
  We turn within.
  We stop seeking others approval as we were born with all the approval we will ever need.
  We are willing to make ourselves available to God so that we might somehow make a difference in this lifetime.
  We are eagerly ready to walk where we are guided.
  We know that our Final Battle is close.

By Joseph Anthony Campbell

We are always loved and protected.

We are always loved and protected.

"I have always loved you." The Prophet Malachi recounts God as declaring. (Malachi 1:2) [12]

God always loves us. Always protects us.

God takes care of the judgement of all men and women.

We learn that the Eternal resides within.

That the material world is a shadow.

That the Eternal exists in a different dimension to it.

We meet Eternity.

We realise that it is not for God to align with us.

That it is us who must align with God.

God is constant and fixed in place.

It is us who are inconstant and move.

We realise that our real enemy is fear itself.

That fear belongs to the darkness. That they are one and the same.

That the darkness strives with the light for the control of our hearts, our minds and our very souls.

---

[12] Malachi 1:2 (New Standard Revised Version)

The Road to the Kingdom.

Be prepared to let go of all that you fear to lose.

Be prepared to let go of all that you fear to lose.
    Nothing that is eternal can be lost.
    We are eternal.
    Fear has corroded our lives.
    It has been created through the fabricated lies of our oft diseased minds.
    Fear cannot survive when we are present in the moment.
    Fear cannot survive when we are aware that it is a lie whispered to us by the darkness.
    Fear cannot surpass our Faith, which we have refined upon the Road.
    Fear cannot conquer Love.
    Our armour comprises of our presence, our awareness, our faith and our love.
    We are now ready to partake in our Final Battle with the darkness and the fear that is both within and around us.

By Joseph Anthony Campbell

Chapter 7: We embark upon our Final Battle.

The Road to the Kingdom.

Become who you were born to be.

Become who you were born to be.

The past is an illusion.

Every step upon the Road, each doubt and every battle has led to this moment.

Your life has led to this exact moment.

Right now. Here. Now.

Facing our greatest fears; our greatest enemies, the very darkness itself, we stand firm.

We hope against hope.

We are prepared to sacrifice ourselves for the greater good.

We stand firm to fight for the greater good.

The good in this world that is worth fighting for, despite the overwhelming odds and whether we may fall or not.

Now, we move towards the crown that we are getting closer to and towards the ultimate battle that must be undertaken.

By Joseph Anthony Campbell

Our time has come; this is our destiny!

Our time has come; this is our destiny!

Our enemy and the darkness are one and the same.

The darkness takes on many different forms for each of us and it aims to make us identify with it.

Some of us have much darkness and therefore many 'enemies' to ride to battle against.

Our battle is personal to ourselves.

However, each of us in turn, each and every one of us can emerge victorious from any battle we face, including this Final Battle, this ultimate battle.

We now ride to battle against our greatest enemy; whatever the odds against us.

We plunge into the heart of our own personal abyss, despite the fear we feel.

As we accept the eternal present moment and act fully within it, we lead the fight and encourage those alongside us to fight their greatest battle too.

We do this with God's help.

We charge into the mouth of the darkness.

We charge into the mouth of the darkness.

We continue to fight despite the temptations of the enemy.

Against the seemingly impossible opponent we fight.

We pick up our swords. We plunge into the heart of the abyss once more and even if we are to die in the process; the good we fight for is worthy of our sacrifice.

We will not escape without being wounded.

We face our pain directly.

We have courage, which has created faith and through this faith in God we are empowered.

We are empowered to fight the perceived undefeatable foe.

We realise that we might just be able to defeat the darkness.

The battle may not signify the end of the war but beyond this battleground we can distinguish the open gates of the Kingdom.

By Joseph Anthony Campbell

Death is an illusion.

Death is an illusion.
    Ultimately one event will lead to the dissolution of our physical body.
    However, we know that nothing eternal can be lost.
    We have emerged from the battlefield.
    Some parts of us have passed away but we are now more ourselves than we have ever been.
    We are forever changed.
    We have restored our Souls.
    We experience peace.
    We are transformed.
    Now transcending former realities, we have stopped seeking and arrived at our true destination.
    Our true home.
    The gates of the Kingdom beckon.
    We walk in undeterred.

Chapter 8: Realising the Kingdom.

By Joseph Anthony Campbell

We had met ourselves and found ourselves worthy.

We had met ourselves and found ourselves worthy.

In the Wilderness our journey had begun.

From the Wilderness we had emerged.

Through our training and development in the skills of a Magician, a Lover and a Warrior we had integrated all aspects of ourselves.

We journeyed upon the Road and whilst pausing to reflect we had learned that we need to restore our relationship with our Creator.

We had discovered a whole new relationship with God and with life itself.

In our final battle against our ultimate darkness God had helped us every step of the way and never left us.

We know now that the Kingdom is within us.

We know that only God can crown us.

And that our crowning will be to the benefit of all men and women.

When the crownless become Kings and Queens.

When the crownless become Kings and Queens.
 We are at last crowned.
 Our journey has come to an end.
 We have reached our destination.
 Now we commit to this place and to creating heirs to the Kingdom.
 In our coronation speech we acknowledge those who are far from the Road, on the Road or who have journeyed with us or before us to the Kingdom.
 We declare that the rebuilding of this world must be done together. One brick at a time.
 We know that all people have value, that all people deserve love.
 We know that to make an idol out of any person is to destroy both the worshipper and the object of worship.
 Each soul has equal value and we build the Kingdom for each soul, each participator upon the Road.
 Through the Road to the Kingdom, we realise that we have had a direct experience with eternity itself.

By Joseph Anthony Campbell

We will rejoin those we have lost.

We will rejoin those we have lost.

For we know that nothing is ever really lost.

We know that we are part of the eternal NOW that unfolds always.

Those who have left are not really gone as we will not be, when we depart this moment, this reality.

Have you ever looked at the person that you love, into their eyes and recognised the true singularity that binds us?

We will dwell in this unified bliss and it will be eternal rather than a mere glimpse of paradise.

Having attained the Kingdom, we now re-unite with our true love from whom we did not know if we would be able to return. Or we search for our true companion now and accept nothing less.

We also return to love and be loved by our families, our own and those whom we were raised by and raised with and share our truth with them.

We know that love demands commitment and faithfulness.

We are all one.

We are all one.

This is a truth that we have learnt.

We know that we must all aim to share in the days of peace that are to be found in this Kingdom.

We internalise and integrate all that we have learnt.

We embed this message and the truths that we have learnt into our hearts, our minds, our sinews, our blood, our bones; our very Soul.

We will provide leadership to all who need it and explain to others how they too can reach the Kingdom.

We will provide Love.

We will provide Kindness.

We will provide truth.

All that we have learnt we will share with others.

For within these noble ideals is the code of the Kingdom.

By Joseph Anthony Campbell

We kneel to the Source.

We kneel to the Source, without whom none of this would be possible and continue in a lifetime of service.

We know that we must honour and give thanks to the One who made all things, made the very Road that we have journeyed upon.

The One who wishes for us to join him in the Kingdom.

We do not let the words for this Source divide us.

We use whichever word we want: Power/God/Being/Source/Creator.

We remember that words are simply mere pointers to the ultimate transcendent reality.

We know through our journey upon the Road to the Kingdom that this present moment contains our redemption and salvation within it.

For when we are not present, we are far from God. We are not aligned with God's Grace and Truth.

The Kingdom is within us and we experience it NOW. For the NOW is where God lives eternally.

We have found that this is our home too.

The Road to the Kingdom.

Epilogue.

Dearest reader, I hope that the information contained within this book is as much of a blessing to you as it has been to me.

My own life has mirrored the journey that I have presented to you and the completion of this book signifies my own journey upon the Road to the Kingdom.

For myself, I personally believe that Jesus Christ transcended the world and death itself.

That the Buddha was a man who found complete enlightenment.

The truth does not need anyone to uphold and defend it.

Therefore, I beseech you to deepen the truth that you have already found within or continue to look for it fearlessly.

For all seekers are richly rewarded.

God speed upon the Road.

My sincerest wish is that you have reached the Kingdom and found the King or Queen within.

All the very best always,

Joseph

By Joseph Anthony Campbell

Summer courses 2019!

Thank you for reading this transformative book!

Between the 19th of July to the 8th of September, there will be Weekend and Three-Day intensive "Road to the Kingdom" courses with me Joseph Anthony Campbell in central London in Summer 2019.

Contact me at josephrtk@gmail.com to register your interest in taking part and get great early bird offers on the courses taking place in central London.

Let's travel the Road to the Kingdom together!

Very best wishes always,

Joseph

By Joseph Anthony Campbell

A final message to you; dearest reader.

Realising the Kingdom results in the discovery of vital self-knowledge, of the 'King' or 'Queen' within and then transmitting what we have learnt to others. Our journey and the completion of it and the experience gained therein will then be used to improve the world.

However, it is ultimately a journey of progress rather than perfection and we may have to take the 'Road' again but the advice provided in this book and the basic structure is always the same. It could be broken down into three distinct parts: Departure, Initiation and Realisation. 'Departure' dealt with us venturing forth and leaving the Wilderness. 'Initiation' dealt with the development of our skills as a 'Magician', 'Lover' and 'Warrior' with the ultimate hope of becoming a 'King' or 'Queen' of the 'Kingdom'. 'Realisation' dealt with our journeying upon 'The Road to the Kingdom' and realising ourselves spiritually and then mentally and physically through our 'Final Battle'. Then, when we have realised the 'Kingdom'; the 'King' and 'Queen' within and our 'Mind, Body and Spirit' are all unified within us (albeit only temporarily) we have thus experienced a resurrection, a journey from death to life. We have developed the psychic structures needed to overcome any challenge. There are battles still to be fought that lie ahead (as long as we are breathing) but for now we enjoy this moment. We will eventually return 'home' with the knowledge and the powers that we acquired on our journey which we will then transmit to others.

The Road to the Kingdom.

We will face battles of a lesser degree of intensity than before if we have been rigorously honest with ourselves as to what our "Final Battle" (ultimate battle) really was, when we faced it. However, we will undertake this journey once more in the not too distant future and travel upon the 'Road' once again.

My intent is to change the way we think and for us to envision and create a world where people are increasingly enlightened and this change ultimately begins with ourselves. Through transforming our paradigms, we have created a paradigm shift within ourselves. At times, we find we can now live fully within the present moment.

Ultimately, we have become the person we were born to be; the King or Queen unrealised within. We have become a person who is capable of understanding the miracle of life and of fighting to the last for something we believe in.

God Speed upon the Road!

Your Friend,

Joseph

Printed in Poland
by Amazon Fulfillment
Poland Sp. z o.o., Wrocław